we be theorizin

we be theorizin
black poiēsis no. 1. vol. 44

KENDRA NICOLE BRYANT AYA

Betting on My Black Self
North Carolina

we be theorizin: black poiēsis *no. 1. vol. 44.*
By Kendra N. Bryant Aya

For additional information regarding reproduction and/or book
sales, address BOMBS Publishing at 1221 Edenham Way,
Greensboro, NC 27410 or at bombspublishing@gmail.com.

Visit our website: http://bombspublishing.com

FIRST EDITION, August 2024

ISBN-13: 979-8-9908195-0-4

A note about the book cover—
*The book's cover, designed by Kendra N. Bryant Aya, was
created using Canva. The images of Kente strips on the cover
is not an appropriation of African custom. Instead, the Kente
cloth, a widely known textile produced in West Africa, is used
on the cover as a non-verbal expression of how American
Black folks theorize. Wearing Kente is an expression of Black,
African-American pride. As a fabric African Americans wear
to acknowledge our African ancestry, Kente is a statement of
our royal histories and diasporic happenings. Too, because
Kente making is often regulated to male weavers, the Kente
strips applied to a woman's poetic composition signal Black
woman's deference. And so, it is.*

Acknowledgment of previously published works—

"a poem for Yakini," awarded the 2010-2011 College Language Association's *Margaret Walker Memorial Prize in Creative Writing*

"celebration," first published in *Hooked on the Art of Love: My Call for Soul Work*. Ed. Gary L. Lemons. BookLocker, Inc., 2019

"poem for Henry Ossawa Tanner, Aaron Douglas, Jacob Lawrence, Lois Mailou Jones, Augusta Savage, Palmer C. Hayden, Archibald Motley, Romare Bearden, William H. Johnson, Charles Alston, Elizabeth Catlett, Meta Vaux Warrick Fuller, Horace Pippin, Charles W. White, Faith Ringgold, Emory Douglas, Ernie Barnes, Jean-Michel Basquiat, Kara Walker, Kerry J. Marshall, Barkley L. Hendricks, Kadir Nelson, Hank Willis Thomas, Amy Sherald, Kehinde Wiley, et al.," first published in *Hooked on the Art of Love: My Call for Soul Work*. Ed. Gary L. Lemons. BookLocker, Inc., 2019

"sonnet no. 1 for the Black Lives Matter Movement," first published in *Glass: A Journal of Poetry*, June 17, 2020

"we be theorizin," first published in *"The Inside Light": New Critical Essays on Zora Neale Hurston*. Ed. Dr. Deborah G. Plant. Praeger, 2010

Thank you—

Black Black Black Black Black Black Black culture.
Black poets.
The Harlem Renaissance.
The Black Arts Movement.
Black literature.
Black music—gospel, hip-hop, rhythm & blues.
My English instructors.
The Black educators, counselors, & administrators who
weren't technically assigned to teach, counsel, or see over me
but taught, counseled, & saw over me anyway.
Still teach, counsel, & see over me.
My Black students—fodder & muse.
My Black beta readers—Cyndi Ixchele Friday Aya, Kia
Sanders, Brianna Yancey, and Amber White.
My Black wife Cyndi, Cyndi, Cyndi, my Cyndirelli.
My Black mother, Choling Bryant Walker—master teacher.
Provider. Supporter.
The ancestors without whom there'd be no me. No us.

Thru morning pulses we be theorizin Black life unexpected.

to my kinfolk—

from *Ptah Hotep, Sojourner Truth, & Phillis Wheatley; Claude McKay, Sonia Sanchez, & Amiri; Maya Angelou, Lauryn Hill, & Nikki Giovanni; Alice Walker, June Jordan, &* my *mommy*

"The poetry I wasn't to write is oral by tradition, mass aimed as its fundamental function and motive. Black poetry, in its mainstream is oracular, sermonic, it incorporates the scream shouts and moans and wails of the people inside and outside of the churches. The whispers and the thunder vibrato and staccato of the inside and outside of the people themselves and it wants to be as real as anything else and as accessible as a song—a song about a real world, full of good and evil."

—Amiri Baraka, "New Music, New Poetry,"[1] n.d.

"[P]oetry is not a luxury. It is a vital necessity of our existence. It forms the quality of the light within which we predicate our hopes and dreams toward survival and change, . . .The farthest horizons of our hopes and fears are cobbled by our poems, carved from the rock experiences of our daily lives."

—Audre Lorde, "Poetry Is Not a Luxury,"[2] 1977

"For people of color have always theorized - but in forms quite different from the Western form of abstract logic. And I am inclined to say that our theorizing (and I intentionally use the verb rather than the noun) is often in narrative forms, in the stories we create, in riddles and proverbs, in the play with language, since dynamic rather than fixed ideas seem more to our liking. How else have we managed to survive with such spiritedness the assault on our bodies, social institutions, countries, our very humanity? And women, at least the women I grew up around, continuously speculated about the nature of life through pithy language that unmasked the power relations of their world."

—Barbara Christian, "The Race for Theory,"[3] 1987

contents

part 1.
thru morning pulses

⊙

My first poem was about ants: *Diminutive red and black creatures, grovel upon the table*. I wrote it in Mrs. Mesa's fourth grade English Language Arts class after she invited a white man author to talk to my classmates and me about poetry writing. I reckon it was my first poetry workshop. With thesaurus in hand, I wrote the second line: *Peacefully ensnares a jot of bread*. The thesaurus, this white man poet told us, is a necessary resource that would support our poetry writing— would help us to compose with stronger words, to expand our fourth-grade vocabulary with a loftier lexicon than the rudimentary ones our fourth-grade tongues could fashion, he said. So, with tongue-bending thesauri in hand, my classmates and I wrote poems about nature—that awe-inspiring matter propelling an esoteric composition: *Carefully submitting it to its body*.

In June Jordan's 1989 "The Difficult Miracle of Black Poetry in America,"[4] Jordan affirms Phillis Wheatley's audacity to write poems and to rely on poetry writing as a spiritual source against a new world about which Wheatley was unfamiliar—a new world that hated Blackness, that hated *her*. According to Jordan, who juxtaposes white poets with Black ones so noting Black poets' commitment to poetry writing as social protest, human affirmation, and freedom making:

> [T]he *difficult* miracle of Black poetry in
> America, is that we have been rejected and we
> are frequently dismissed as 'political' or
> 'topical' or 'sloganeering' and 'crude' and
> 'insignificant' because, like Phillis Wheatley,
> we have persisted for freedom. We will write
> against South Africa and we will seldom pen a
> poem about wild geese flying over Prague, or
> grizzlies at the rain barrel under the dwarf

willow trees. We will write, published or not,
however we may, like Phillis Wheatley, of the
terror and the hungering and the quandaries of
our African lives on this North American soil.

In other words, unlike white poets free to write esoteric (read:
meaningless) poetry about nature, Black poets must write
poems with teeth, with a grit that usually pushes them into the
lion's mouth. For Black poets, sayeth the Lorde, "poetry is not
a luxury."

My fourth-grade poem, "Ants," won a blue ribbon at the
county's youth fair; it was the last poem I wrote about a nature
that failed to reveal how and *that* I persist in a country that
knows me subhuman. "Surely i am able to write poems /
celebrating grass and how the blue / in the sky can flow green
or red / and the waters lean against the / chesapeake shore like
a familiar," writes Lucille Clifton. "surely / but whenever i
begin / 'the trees wave their knotted branches / and . . .' why /
is there under that poem always / an other poem?"[5]

I was in Mrs. Krane's 7th grade journalism class when I
watched Maya Angelou deliver "On the Pulse of Morning"
during Bill Clinton's 1993 presidential inauguration. Besides
the rock, the river, the tree, and the final "good morning"
Angelou recited, I understood not a word of her poem. But I
felt it. I *felt* Angelou's courage, her commitment to liberation
and human rights. I *felt* her sadness for those of us, including
herself, who have been thingified and othered within
America's democratic project. And I *felt* her spiritual striving
toward and hope for America's humanity.

Although my 7th grade self lacked the intellectual capacity to
grasp Angelou's inaugural poem, I knew Angelou's message
was not just about nature, per se, but people's courage to be *in
the nature* of their humanity—to be Black. Woman. Native.
Alive. To just be and to love others in their being. Human.

2

Standing in the cold of a Washingtonian winter, wrapped in a blue peacoat Oprah Winfrey gifted her, Maya Angelou showed the country how to persist within tumultuous weather. And I wanted to be like *her*—to pen poems reminding Black folks to rise, and rise again—a Black resurrection. A force of nature.

Good morning.

SOS no. 1: tanka for Black freedom fighters
inspired by Amiri Baraka,[6] June Jordan,[7] & Kia Sanders

Ey yo!

callin Òrìṣàs[8]:
Ògún,[9] Ṣàngó,[10] Aganju[11]
Ọṣun,[12] Ọlọrun![13]
come out come out wherever you are
& strengthen us w/àṣẹ[14]

a song flung up to heaven[15]: poem for Maya Angelou

who will honor her with poems
as much as she's honored us?

she—
our bodacious black woman poet
our mother, grandmother, sister
our friend

she—
who rose thru racism & rape
speechlessness & humiliation
teenage pregnancy & segregation

she—
who loved Shakespeare just as much as Dunbar
who privileged teachers & librarians
who walked with Martin & Malcolm

who will honor her with poems
as much as she's honored us?

she claimed we're phenomenal women
she encouraged us to rise
she united us on morning's pulses

she—
who stood in her grandmother's genius
while affirmed in her mother's love
offered herself for borrowing, for she knew: nobody,
no, nobody can make it our here alone

& we—quite gratefully—took her:
into our churches
into our schools
into our Presidential Inaugurations & United Nations

we—
printed her in textbooks

5

featured her in films
taped her onto our bathroom mirrors

we—
sat her on our bookshelves
placed her in our memories
fixed her in our hearts
so tho we may be caged birds
we have the fire to sing

her traveling shoes became our own
we gatheredtogether in her name
we sung & swung & got merry like Christmas
for life didn't frighten us at all
cause the stars weren't lonesome beside her light

who will honor her with poems
as much as she's honored us?

she—
our brazen black woman poet
our amazing peace
the heart of a woman

she—
who got her cool drink of water 'fore she died
who needs nothing else for her journey now
whose wings fit her perfectly well

trumpets sound
shakers sing
a song's flown up to heaven!

found poem: Langston, Mari, & Dolores
from The Harlem Renaissance to The Black Arts Movement

She was tired.

movin throughout the land
like a moonbeam,
takin care of those
other than herself[16]

She wanted out
of this earthly experience

to explode/in the majesty of her oneness[17]
a trillion Black stars
tripping the light
into milky ways of dark matter—

a sheltering

like a hut built near the Congo
lulling her to sleep[18]

poem for the 276 Nigerian girls[19]

I sit in the comfort of my home:
    a creative space
    a free space
    a safe space
where I can be anything I want:
    poet, painter, teacher, thinker
Woman.
a Woman on the loose
I stumble over books
falling in philo-sophy w/
    Audre Lorde & Maya Angelou
    Alice Walker & Giovanni
    Lucille Clifton & Margaret Walker
    Zora Neale Hurston & Emecheta
    Sonia Sanchez & Toni Morrison
    Elaine Brown & June Jordan
& if we are the ones we have been waiting for
how long will it take us to save each of you?

276
Black girls
    a mother's daughter
    an auntie's niece
    a brother's sister
    a child's friend
    a teacher's student—
no different than the students I teach to know
themselves in Harriet, Sojourner, Winnie, & Coretta—
to know themselves as ancient as Aminatu[20]

I sit in the comfort of my home
free to be anything I want:
    scholar, journalist, activist, dreamer
    Woman.

a Black woman
a Black lesbian woman
on the loose wishing for ur freedom
wondering how Black men who know their Black
mother's breasts can be so hateful

deaf to ur songs, ur poems, ur prayers
deaf to the divine drumming in you

I sit in the comfort of my home
& I listen.

Trying to hear God over their hatred
        leaning toward love
        combatting fury
        nurturing compassion
        forestalling violence
        favoring violence—a hardhearted kill:
their blood for ur freedom
276 times over

mad.

I have only a pen too dull for fighting.

poem for Henry Ossawa Tanner, Aaron Douglas, Jacob Lawrence, Lois Mailou Jones, Augusta Savage, Palmer C. Hayden, Archibald Motley, Romare Bearden, William H. Johnson, Charles Alston, Elizabeth Catlett, Meta Vaux Warrick Fuller, Horace Pippin, Charles W. White, Faith Ringgold, Emory Douglas, Ernie Barnes, Jean-Michel Basquiat, Kara Walker, Kerry J. Marshall, Barkley L. Hendricks, Kadir Nelson, Hank Willis Thomas, Amy Sherald, Kehinde Wiley, et al.
for Dr. Gary L. Lemons (d. 2024)

flat forms, hard edges, & abstract geometry
rhythm a Negro life of respect & affection
raising the possibility of rebellion explored
thru human contact & cooperation

painting w/depth & color—
we fashion art compelling recognition
of a reality remembering romance
reaching as far back as hieroglyphs canvassing
pyramid walls

we are not lampblacked anglo-saxons[21]
but Negro artists
standing on top of the mountain
free w/in ourselves[22]
to magnify goodness &Truth[23] by staging Barack
Obama inside a paradise professing divinity[24]

Black is beautiful.

& w/each brush stroke
we portray Black folk
whose souls invoke
visual mythologies of power
ensuring hue/manity
mid landscapes
void of color

tanka: dance of the dissident daughter[25]

goddess, great mother
mary, oshun, yemaya
eve, mungu, hokmah—
her back is a turtle's shell
balancing the universe

a poem for Yakini

& I think about how beautifully Black you are
shimmering like Shug Avery's shimmy
brighter than Celie's smile after Shug kisses her on the
lips & I wonder:

if you kiss me on the lips,
will I shine too?
or will I hide my face
ashamed of ur humanity?

but you don't see me staring at you wanting to be in ur
body to know ur thoughts
to feel ur skin to hold ur hand & climb w/you to a
mountain's top

& I think of you in church on Easter Sunday wearing a
too pink pink dress revealing scrawny Black legs
scarred by last year's chicken pox & wounded by
limbs of the oak tree shading grandmother's front
porch a place for drinking moonshine playing cards
watching passersby pass by

& ur sitting in church staring at that white jesus
knowing he's not ur savior
basking in big women wearing feathered hats crying
jesus's name questioning how grandmothers can trust
a god they've never seen & why do you have to recite
a resurrection speech when you'd rather lay out dead
in the sun?

& I see you growing thru hopscotch & double dutch
coconut milk & vegetable bean patties wearing thick
Black pigtails in summer's heat eating a seeded
watermelon not caring if they call you pickaninny
because ur Black and Black is beautiful matter
unmoved in integrated schools where Black teachers
are rarely visible to show Black students freedom

12

fighting riding in the name of heroes unsung but not
forgotten despite history's lessons that aren't ur story
you daydream of Marcus Garvey & Booker T.
Washington gather ur bootstraps & march all the way
to the Motherland searching for the Dahomey
Amazons

& I see ur Afro wearing dashiki flaunting self who's
changed her name so *Black* rings off the tongues of
those who call you & maybe white folks will
holyghost when they hear how beautiful *Yakini* sounds
intone ur name beg you to save them from
boomeranged lynchings recalling hoover lynch &
crow cawing a revolution Black folks won't be afraid
of

& I see you mothering daughters braiding hair sewing
dresses mending wounds singing "To be Young Gifted
& Black" teaching them how to be humane under
inhumane conditions Big Momma standing on a
mountain top overseeing w/out being an overseer gray
locs signaling wisdom each strand be salvation you
bless them

& when I lay me down praying the moon doesn't turn
blood red & the stars won't fall to the ground making
earth void of light, I see you reading the palm of your
own hand until I fall asleep

the grand dragon reads from an instructional manual on environmentalism

let me tell you how to do it from the beginning:

before the body
you gotta secure the rope
tied into a knot
forming a loop at its end
half hitch, figure eight, bowline

tuck bight, pull it thru
the rabbit comes out the hole
wrap around, go back down
yonder / into wet wooded
white oak & poplar landscapes

give *thanks for the tree*
whose bark gave us rope to knot
its branch bears torched weight
heavy enuf to break

14

sonnet no. 1 for the Black Lives Matter Movement

Black Lives Matter don't make Black lives matter
when white robes in blue suits judge & jury.
"We want justice!" sounds like Babel's chatter,
yet the world questions Black rage & fury.
What's not outrageous 'bout Black bodies lynched?
We're target practice in a new Jim Crow;
& tho we march w/fists erect & clenched,
it may all come down to one deadly blow.
& w/each swing, we will call out their names—
Trayvon, Eric,[26] Sandra,[27] & Emmett Till—
we'll fight 'til we call each Black body slain.
& since we're divine, it'll be in God's will
to live thru Nat Turner,[28] scrap to the end!
Come what may come 'til liberation wins!

sonnet no. 2 for the Black Lives Matter Movement

bring the dogs motherfucker[29] bring the dogs
if you bad, bring yo water hoses too
but be ready cause we won't die like hogs
we gone let it do what it's bound to do
we aint gone be pressed 'gainst no walls dyin[30]
we'll be too enraged w/fightin back
fists—& even bullets—might be flyin
but won't be no Black bodies bein stacked
so bring yo dogs motherfucker, bring em
if you bad, bring yo water hoses too
America's 'bout to pay for her sins
when y'all chicken heads come home to roost
come hell or high water, we gone right ur wrongs
& noose-knottin Black folks will roar freedom songs

sonnet no. 3 for the Black Lives Matter Movement

if the people could fly,[31] they'd fly from here
like the Africans fled their offenders,
releasing pain & surrendering fear
existing in their absolute splendor.
if the people could fly, they'd fly beyond
red horizons & cloud's silver linings,
between the sky where silence is song
& living doesn't feel more like dying.
but the people can't fly; their wings are clipped,
their bosoms sore & brutally battered;[32]
so they take to the streets yesteryear's script,
& in protest they chant: "Black lives matter!"
"Black lives matter!" "Black lives matter!" "Black
lives—" get madder else yo revolution will be
televised

the mourning of trees: a ballad for Southern Black women lynched[33]
written in a poetry workshop with Marilyn Nelson

We'se got dis burden we cain't break,
so we cry inside de win'.
Sorrow so heavy are leaves they shake;
its weight be in are bend.

Crawls from are roots;
gnaws at are fruit;
its stench stinks up de air.
We'se got dis burden we cain't break
despite are flowers flair.

Folk don't quite know we mournin;
it's lak dey jes fo'got.
Black bodies strung burned up are trunks
& lef' on us tuh rot.

De worl' it jes go on
bout are hardness an' grayd strenf.
Are 'durance an' stability
be talked about at length.

Folks plant us near still waters;
not one of us be moved—
lak spirited Black womins
who got dey share of blues.

Nevuh mine we'se of'en wuhshipped;
We'se grayd big tok'ns tuh some.
We aid in stoppin' climate change,
but we ratha kingdom come.

Are prayers be rustlin' leaves
you'se hear befo uh storm.
Dey be are nervous conditions
dat beckons bad weather's form.

Leaves wail upon de win's
tuh tear open de sky.
Its wounds conjuh de nimbus
tuh gathuh an' multiply.

Tuh deluge down upon us
uh storm dat snaps are trunks,
an' we fall lak Roman's Empire,
an' de earfth—she runs uhmuck.

She thunduhs an' makes light'nin'
'til hurricanes be born,
from which tornadoes thrash about
bellowin' doze we mourn:

Maria Smith[34] &
Milly Thompson[35]
Anna Cowan[36] &
Eliza Wood[37]
Harriet Finch[38] &
Mary Hollenbeck[39]
we woulda saved ya if we could.

Gracy Blanton[40] &
Ella Williams[41]
Roxie Elliot[42]
& Louisa Carter[43]
Mary Motlow[44]
& Mollie Smith[45]
yo tears made standin' harduh.

Marion Howard[46] &
Felicia Francis[47]
Catherine Matthews[48]
& Hannah Kearse[49]
Emma Fair[50] &
Amanda Franks[51]
we praise ya in all de earfth.
Dora Baker[52] &

Lizzie Pool[53]
Ella Charles[54]
& Charlotte Morris[55]
Ann Boston[56]
& Alice Green[57]
we regret u'se hanged befo us.

Emma Wideman[58] &
Meta Hicks[59]
Laura Nelson[60]
& Stella Long[61]
Minnie Ivory[62]
& Ida McCray[63]
how kin we right dis wrong?

Crawls from are roots;
gnaws at are fruit;
its stench stinks up de air.
We'se got dis burden we cain't break
despite are flowers flair.

Sorrow so heavy are leaves they shake;
its weight be in are bend.
We'se got dis burden we cain't break,
so we gives it to de win.

poem for the 18-year-old students I teach in first-year composition
a haiku narrative assignment from Saturday's poetry workshop requiring participants to compose a poem using seven words

young black rioters
be talkin **revolution**
unchanged in they selves

esteems like ego
trippin toward a **freedom**
of self-indulgence

too smug for **water**
guns blazing in-di(g)-nation
conjured by white rage

it's **intentional**—
a capitalist surplus
branding them "other"

*father forgive them
for they know not what they do
to meek embodied*

Black kids **united**
in the struggle for justice
be a bout it folk

no **adult learner**
weathered by experience
can alter their course

part 2.
we be theorizin

⊙

In 2023, Hip-Hop celebrated its 50th anniversary. Developed in 1973 in Bronx, New York, DJ Kool Herc is most often credited as its founder, for he revolutionized Black music—its funk, soul, and disco—by using multiple turntables to extend its percussive breaks, thereby extending the song's beat to which Black and brown listeners danced. "Hard times require furious dancing," says Alice Walker.[64] Thus, and perhaps unwittingly so, Kool Herc provided young folks coming to age during America's 1960s countercultural movement a New York city dancefloor where they could wild out to beating drums—like West African dancers in heat. That Bronx dance floor, which ultimately evolved into a cultural movement that now crosses seven continents, was about seven miles from the Black Arts Movement's (BAM) Harlem location.

Organized by poet Amiri Baraka in 1965, the BAM—out of which spoken word came and, inarguably, rapping (also called MCing)—was the modern Harlem Renaissance. Artists, particularly poets, answered Langston Hughes's 1926 call and response to the respectability politics of that era. Hughes was 25 years old when he wrote:

> We younger Negro artists who create now
> intend to express our individual dark-skinned
> selves without fear or shame. If white people
> are pleased we are glad. If they are not, it
> doesn't matter. We know we are beautiful.
> And ugly too. The tom-tom cries and the tom-
> tom laughs. If colored people are pleased we
> are glad. If they are not, their displeasure
> doesn't matter either. We build our temples
> for tomorrow, strong as we know how, and we
> stand on top of the mountain, free within
> ourselves.[65]

Like Langston Hughes, whose poetry reflects the blues-singing Negro whose working-class status made him a more authentic, therefore, beautiful figure, Amiri Baraka and other BAM poets (re)produced a literary movement reflecting their social environment, while countering social norms—chiefly those denigrating Black folks. As the "aesthetic and spiritual sister of Black Power,"[66] BAM was a radical movement during which poets were spoken word artists akin to street-preachin Malcolm X; they floated and stung like Muhammad Ali— baaaaaaad as they wanna be.

Spoken word artists like The Last Poets and Haki R. Madhubuti, Nikki Giovanni, and Sonia Sanchez ushered rapping into Hip Hop; arguably, they pioneered (and/or systematized) rapping. As one of the four (general) elements of Hip-Hop culture, *rapping* is defined as "a vocal style in which the artist speaks lyrically and rhythmically, in rhyme and verse, generally to an instrumental or synthesized beat,"[67] which BAM's poets were already doing: reciting their political poems to a djembe, in front of a live gospel choir, to their own beat-making vocals (read: *beat boxing*).

So, when Gil Scot Heron recites, "A rat done bit my sister Nell / With whitey on the moon / Her face and arms began to swell / And whitey's on the moon";[68] or Amiri Baraka asks for "'poems that kill.'"/ Assassin poems, Poems that shoot /Guns. Poems that wrestle cops into alleys / And take their weapons leaving them dead";[69] or Nikki Giovanni proclaims: "I turned myself into myself and was / jesus / men intone my loving name / All praises All praises / I am the one who would save,"[70] that Black poet is rapping. Her heart is the djembe maintaining the beat and tempo of her spoken text—both of which is pounded into the ether expressing Black life, validating Black being.

In other words, when a Black poet communicates their humanity upon an America hardened with an -ism that aims to kill us, that uttered sound *reeling with power*[71]— incomprehensible or not—is always a rap.

I am (because they were)

beautifully Black women
sheathed in deep dark splendidly smooth skin
beautifully Black like plums
breasts dangling hanging but not strange fruit
feeding beautiful Black babies
pleasuring fathers who sowed their seeds:
bodies strong & stern
limbs long & lanky
lips thick & full
nose broad & wide
eyes bright & round—sun discs set inside an Ancient
Wonder
brass & beads silver & gold adorn & adore them
their hair—a beautifully kinky coiled coarse mangled
mass of majesty
the epitome of their strength
Sampson mocks him & Hagar was made in her image.
She—
stolen
stripped
drug across brazen bronze beaches
reaching out for her father brother uncle
holding onto her mother daughter auntie.
they are all there.
naked. hopeless helpless
haplessly beholding each other
wanting to say something
needing to do something
wailing out something
clenching the bit restricting free speech
they reach.
but land inside the belly of beasts
& I am them shipped overseas
stacked one
      on top of the other

            on top of the other
            on top of the other.
breathin ingestin prayin survivin dyin
in each other's feces
in each other's urine
in each other's vomit
in each other's spit
in each other's blood
stacked one
            on top of the other
            on top of the other
            on top of the other
& they waded in water
some waitin on Moses
some sang Negro spirituals—undergoing hypnosis
for toilin plantations
endurin segregation
witnessin lynch attempt to kill a nation
but they sang Negro spirituals
remainin humane under inhumane situations.
& Nat Turner must've been my daddy
cause I'm the revolt headed north
keepin the movement moving.

I am Harlem & the Renaissance
paintin writin jazzin dancin
ownin my own
creatin community
livin life thru the arts
& bein beautifully brilliant
& bein beautifully Black—a masterpiece in of myself.
I am *once riding in old Baltimore heart-filled head-
filled w/glee*[72]
& *they seemed to be staring at the dark, but their eyes
were watching God*[73]

28

& they were told to go tell it on the mountain top that
they'll face the murderous cowardly pack pressed to
the wall dying but fighting back[74]
I am Zora Neale Hurston & Claude McKay
Countee Cullen & Langston Hughes
'cause *I too sing America*
& when they see how beautifully Black I am, they
won't tell me to go eat in the kitchen.[75]
I am James Baldwin & *the fire next time*
Richard Wright & *the native son*
I am Alice Walker & who can walk by the color purple
& not see God in it? See God in me?
I am Nina Simone & Mississippi Goddamn
Ella Fitzgerald & a tisk it a task it
I am Josephine Baker & Dizzy Gillespie
Sarah Vaughn & Cab Calloway—
doo doo dee wop scat dat doo wop doo wop.
I am Pearl Bailey & Billie Holiday
strange fruit on strange trees
I am Lena Horne & Ethel Waters
Bojangles & Fats Waller
I am Jacob Lawrence & William Johnson
the souls of Black folks & W.E.B.
Jean Toomer & Booker T.
& I am gatherin myself by my bootstraps
& keepin the movement moving
in Cotton Clubs & the Apollo Theater
speakeasies & rent parties.

I am freedom fighters & freedom riders
revolutionaries & civil rights martyrs
my father / is Nelson Mandela & Medgar Evers
Malcolm X & Steven Biko
Stokley Carmichael.
He's Huey P. Newton & Frederick Douglass
Bayard Rustin & Ruchelle Magee

a New Jersey Turnpike & Sundiata
history in textbooks don't tell all about em
unsung heroes but never forgotten
like my mother who fought right beside them.
I am daughter of Choling
Myrlie & Coretta
Angela Davis, Fannie Lou, & Ella
Elaine Brown & Sister Souljah
I am Rosa.
& those four little girls in the Birmingham Church
who didn't know they were targets at birth
& bein Black was like bein cursed
a stain upon a whitened Earth
that gave us blue-eyed Jesus
a blonde Jesus
a white Jesus
who resembled the white men who hated us.
but we turned the other cheek & embraced our pink
sisters & brothers
some considered nigger lovers
standin in arms singin *we shall overcome*.

for we know love will overcome everything.

I am the Little Rock Nine
bus boycotts & sit-ins
I am the dream that Martin envisioned
the SCLC & the NAACP
I am the Black Panther Party
a revolutionary holdin graspin bearin arms
walkin down Oakland threatenin to harm
any pig that gets in the way
of my revolutionary thoughts
& my directin Black people
on revolutionary walks.
& I say—

say it out loud! I'm Black & I'm proud!
& I say—
Black is beautiful!
& I say—
power to the people!
& I say—
to be young gifted & Black!
& I say—
lift ev'ry voice & sing!
& I dare anybody to silence me.
& because The Last Poets said the revolution won't be
televised
I am attempting to provoke an uprise
sing to those who welcome change
who invite it
embrace it
& want to enterup white America w/it.
I say—
come on & go w/me
put on yo travelin shoes
& let's freedom ride
cause I am Plessy v. Ferguson
& Brown v. Board
I am the North Star & the Drinkin Gourd
I am Harriet Tubman who laid down the pavement
for the movement.
so let's collect all the brilliantly blazing Black people
& charge them to keep the movement movin
& encourage no one to stay still.

I am illllllllllllllllll!
like hip-hop & shell tops
break dance & be-pop
electric slide & the robot
the chicken head & pop-lock
I am *fight the power*[76]

31

& *100 miles & runnin runnin runnin runnin runnin* [77]
I am *purple rain* & Stephanie Mills
Afrika Bambaataa & Sugar Hill
I am Fat Albert & the Junk Yard Gang
ladies first[78] & *cop killer*[79]
self-destruction[80] public enemy & *thriller*
I am a gangSTARrrrr
wearing jeri curls & faded tops
cross colors & reeboks
I am east coast & west coast niggas who forgot
that our ancestors were stolen stripped & drug across
brazen bronze beaches
sold & shipped overseas
stacked one
        on top of the other
        on top of the other
        on top of the other
makin the way so we can have freedom.
I am now-a-laters & lemon heads
pickled pig's feet & pickled eggs
the kind that soaks in a big ol jar
full of red / vinegar
sittin on the countertop in Perry's corner convenient
store.
I am nigga please & that's my nigga
hopscotch & I left my boyfriend at the candy store
I am everybody singin dancin to the music while I sit
in the back bedroom
wantin wishin tryin to figure out how I can ease my
way into the livin room
& cut a rug w/my parents & their adult friends
pretendin to be a hippie—
a flower girl smokin reefer & makin memories.
I am *Yo MTV Raps! different strokes & good times*
doin the butt the alf & bump-n-grind
I am Black History Month & reports on Jesse Jackson

I am aaaaction[81]
& not knowin the rest of the words
cause I am an American Black
& the lyrics are in patois. My English is never enuf.
I am collard greens & chitterlings
fried chicken & turkey wings
Arsenio Hall & afro picks
double dutch & you-are-not-it.
I am *Ebony Jet* & *Word Up* magazine
coconut yoo-hoo & Muslims sellin beeeeeeeean /
piiiiiies
I am the movement makin sho Black doesn't die
like biiiiiiirds in the skyyyyyyyy
weeeee flyyyyyy highhhhhh.

so throw yo fists in the ai-errrrr
& wave em like ya just don't cay-errrrr
& if ya Blackity Black
yo Black is all that
let me hear ya scream—

oh yeaaaaaaa!

celebration
after reading bell hooks' "remembered rapture:
the writer at work," 1999

    we
    write here

    claiming our space in choreographed words
    patterned to move spirit
    thru morning pulses[82] & hanging fire[83]

    ego tripping[84]
    into the majesty of our oneness
    our coming together in a comingtogetherness[85]
    we   real cool[86]
    phenomenal women[87]
    tall as a cypress[88]
    having found our mothers' gardens[89]
    & taking root there
    where bein alive & bein a woman & bein colored
    is no more a metaphysical dilemma to be conquered[90] /
    for

    we
    write here,
    I say

    entering our shadow self
    thru words of fire[91]
    forging spiritual character
    that makes complexity clear
    & reality confrontable

    composing under soprano skies[92]
    we breakin silence
    throwin down
    gettin ovah
    & high steppin
    into a movement in Black[93]

that promises a second generation of courage
a people loving freedom
& a beauty full of healing[94]

born in a bed of good lessons[95]
we
write here
are the ones we have been waiting for[96]

so you—
over there—
come here!
come fold urself in these words unfolding rapture
& be made new

soul talk

I. Blessed are they that moan
when they lied to you
& took you from the land they're *still* taking from
stripped you of ur titles
of ur communities
of ur liberties
of ur majesties
when they stole ur rituals & tried to steal ur soul,
you moaned.

when they stripped you of ur clothing
took from you ur jewelry
lacerated ur beautiful Black skin
placed chains around ur necks
cuffs around ur limbs
a bit between ur teeth & ur tongue so you could not
cry out,
you moaned.

when they packed you in the belly of their ships
stacked you one
          on top of the other
          on top of the other
          on top of the other
you lay in feces
you lay in vomit
you lay in blood
you lay in tears
& while you lay there
one
          on top of the other
          on top of the other
          on top of the other,
you moaned.

when they sold you on auction blocks
separated you from husbands & wives
        daughters & sons
        aunties & uncles
        brothers & sisters
        grandparents—
when they tried to separate you from ur self
ur body ur mind ur heart,
you moaned.

& when they made you concubine & mammy
cook & sharecropper
snitch & maid
overseer & messenger
driver & nigger
property,
you moaned.

but above ur moaning, you sang "Follow the Drinking
Gourd" & "Down by the Riverside"
you danced the cake walk & strummed the fiddle
shucked the corn & boiled the hog
you learned ur letters & read—defiantly—to ur babies
& you mothered theirs as if they were ur very own
You—bigger than Mary—
coddled their white children & moaned them to sleep

torn & battered
defiled & denigrated
you went the distance in ur heart
& recreated ur self—new language new religion
new being
never allowing ur spirit to die
centering urself thru fervent prayer
forgiving them of their trespasses
you moaned

& because of ur will, I am here.

II. & after the moaning
when they called you ugly, you cried,
Black is beautiful
when they hanged ur body, you said,
Keep hope alive
when they dehumanized you, you claimed,
I am somebody
when they denied ur vote, you declared,
Power to the people
when they burned crosses on ur lawn, you preached,
I have a dream
when they pit you against each other, you chanted,
United we stand
when they bombed ur churches, you sang,
We shall overcome
when they spat in ur face, you said,
Keep ur eyes on the prize
when they blasted you w/water hoses, you insisted,
I shall not be moved
when they said you couldn't, you said,
Yes we can!

& you did.

fired up!
& ready to go
w/arms locked akimbo
you went toward activism
strapped w/clarity & calm
compassion & peace
forgiveness
& turn the other cheek
ur movement kept the movement moving

& because of ur will, I am here.

III. We Became Hip Hop
w/boom boxes & basement parties
Black folks be the new John Gotti
of American popular culture

no vultures clothed in hoods & robes
can take away what the Negro knows
especially when it's in his soul
to be a natural genius

so pledge allegiance to hip hop
who's got its roots in jazz & be-pop
from Negro spirituals, ragtime, & blues
it's the source that expresses the hue
in the quality of being human

fumin rhyme & alliteration
tellin stories thru narration
w/hyperbole & personification
no need for abstracts (some moderations)
when tryin to arouse a sleepin nation
& spur a change of heart

yo! hip hop is art
& it's spittin the truth
dressed in jeans & Timberland boots
tatted up skin & AKOO suits
commonly mos def defines its roots
graffiti & break dancin be makin that loot
& there's nothin small about it

so let's shout it!
when I say *hip*, you say *hop*
hip—

hip—
yea, you don't stop.

cause hip hop takin back dreams deferred
& it's takin over the whole wide world
bringin clarity to what was blurred
fuckwhatchuheard
it's all of that
it's debunking the myths that dehumanized Black
cause we more than niggas slingin crack
we built America on bended backs
& now we stand on shoulders

standin on shoulders of genius passed
we passin the mic like passin that grass
blowin up speakers like blowin that grass
burnin up airwaves like burnin that grass
sellin out records like sellin that grass
poppin that coochie & droppin that ass

yea, hip hop is sometimes crass
& expectedly so since it comes from jazz
but listenin to rap is like bein in class
cause rappers be droppin that knowledge
have ur ass thinkin you in college

one time for Kanye West & Je-sus walks
just because it's my jam
& hip-hop music is what I am
from slave ships to kingships
no longer constrained by bits & whips
hip hop maintains we are the shit
we phat we ill we hype we hip
& love's the language falls off our lips

we are (w)rapped up in rainbows.[97]

we be theorizin
after reading Barbara Christian's 1987 "The Race for Theory" in Dr. Shirley Toland-Dix's 20th Century African American Literature course

They thought we was over here shuckin & jivin
when all the while we been theorizin
How else you think Black folk survivin
They trytuh keep us down
but we keeps on thrivin
Can't no oppression keep us from strivin
They trytuh break our souls
but we keeps on smilin
& thru grins & lies
we master guisin
Gotta be a trickster for humanizin
But we'll wear the mask
cause we be theorizin

So right on Zora Neale
Write on
Right on W. DuBois
Write on
Right on Booker T.
Write on
Cause we been watchin God
while they been in the dark
The souls of Black folks
produce the purest heart
& our plantin seeds
is just a start
See we sowin wisdom
w/literary arts
& thru performances
that's how we impart
the theory they claim rename & bogart
our Black existence is avant-garde

& our future makin be off the charts
So right on Langston Hughes
Write on
Right on Tananarive Due
Write on
Right on Richard Wright
Write on
Right on James Baldwin
Write on
Cause the Negro speaks of rivers
in between the weary blues
He's the native son
the outsider if she choose
& if Beale Street could talk
it would share some news
cause we've gone a piece of the way
in our travelin shoes
& tho our cuttin the rug might seem our muse
we be theorizin & maskin the clues
So right on Nella Larsen
Write on
Right on Countee Cullen
Write on
Right on Claude McKay
Write on
Cause just as quick as sand
we can change our tune
We speak in vernaculars
they call us a coon
But once they're out of our way
& have left the room
out comes Harlem wine
& intellectuals bloom
& when the Harlem dancer makes her body croon
that's our theory that esoterically looms

42

So talk that talk money
& walk that walk
Black feeling & judgment compels them to gawk
It's our colorful brilliance
that makes them balk
at the notion that we be a theory

Cause we be theorizin
in our baptizin
In churches & clubs
we signifyin
Gospel jazz blues got us cryin
Oral traditions keep us from dyin
We flyin on tryin
We hypnotizin
& dance floors are our silver linin's
Creatin the arts keep us glidin
So we paintin faith & buildin horizons
Keepin hope alive & eyes on prizes
& writin poetry makes us the wisest
We are the ones we been waitin for

We soar . . .
Like . . . birds . . . in . . . the sky . . .

So high five
Giovanni & Gwendolyn Brooks
Nina Simone, Alice Walker, bell hooks
Malcolm X & Leopold Senghor,
Houston Baker, Toni Morrison, & Lorde
Martin Luther King,
Frantz Fanon, Cornel West
Jamaica Kincaid, Lauryn Hill, & Mos Def
Angela Davis, Elaine Brown, & Assata
John Hope Franklin & Afrika Bambaataa
Marcus Garvey & Henry Louis Gates

Aime Cesaire, Soyinka, & Daisy Bates
Huey Newton, Ntozake, & Baraka
All givin life to Barack Obama!
See our theorizin
be our salvation
thru the Middle Passage & their plantations
thru jim crow laws & humiliation
cointelpro & subjugation
Our theorizin so bright it's blazin

We are the light that gives them life

Blacker than the Blackest night
We the blues on the left
& the funk on the right
magical & dy-nO-mite—
we are the world's good time

Cause we be theorizin
which is our uprisin
No reparations, but we enterprisin
Creatin life to keep from dyin
Singin dancin paintin & writin
We giants

& our hue gives the world humanity.

a response to King's "An Experiment in Love"[98]
for the first-year writing students who took my composition
course on King's rhetoric

it be that—
understanding good will for all humans love   that
overflowing spontaneous unmotivated love   that
disinterested uninhibited creative love   that
I get my oms from my poems
so, I write them love   that
expression of Creator in creations love   that
I create & be Jesus cause I am God love

it be Grandma's quilts & Grandma's hands
planting roses in barren lands
writing novels that end up banned
making mandalas in open sand

it be that—
groundless I love you solely for the sake
of you love   that
God is operating in my human heart
so all there is *is* love   that
neighbor regarding concern
only for the other love   that

there is no distinction between a friend
& a foe love   that
raging 'gainst property
vs raging 'gainst people love   that
turn the other cheek—be still. be calm. love   that
be strong. be faith. be hope & peace love   that
we could have killed 'em by the hundreds
but we chose nonviolence love   that
we suckled white babies tho they raped us love   that
we created delicacies out of their garbage love   that
we created our language
tho they banished our tongue love   that
we created religion out of their churches love

& we bowed at their feet
tho we were kings & queens love

it be that—
response to the need for belonging love   that
Samaritan who helped the Jew in Jericho love   that
seeking to preserve create community love   that
will to forgive restore & resurrect love   that
I am more than ur keeper, I am ur sister love   that
Holy Ghost moving silencing ego love   that
quiet love.   that
still love.   that
mindfulness practice
meeting contemplation love   that
falling into the depths of my soul love   that
I am present. I am here. I am alive love   that
breathing becomes easy so I easily breathe love that
more than me love   that
we love   that
conscious love   that

agape love.

part 3.
Black life unexpected

⊙

The human condition about which Black poets write their poems have often been composed to meet the "odd demand" of proving our civilization[99]—of our humanity. Though narratives of a Black life unexpected are familiar *still*, poetry offers new ways of making old ideas *felt*.[100] For instance, in a 2009 PBS interview, Sonia Sanchez explains how she discovered the traditional Japanese haiku in New York City's 8th Street Bookshop—and in finding it, she found herself. She tells the PBS interviewer that as she practiced writing the haiku, traditionally about a pristine nature, she reconceptualized it as a *blues haiku*—an intersection of blues music and Japanese haiku, "funked up" with Black English. According to Sanchez, although the traditional haiku may be, for example, a representation of a beautiful sunset, the *blues haiku* expresses that in nature which has been untouched—that which is "not as simple as we are," says Sanchez: "When the sun sets, night sets in, and the other side of the haiku is what happens at night." Sanchez develops her point thusly: "When you write a haiku about a caterpillar crawling on a leaf, it [the haiku] doesn't talk about how it's [the caterpillar's] gonna eat up that leaf, and the leaf disappears."[101] As such, Sanchez's *blues haiku*, is the "other" story. The "othered" story.

Sanchez claims that in writing and speaking the haiku, specifically in the one breath it requires, the haiku keeps people alive, for it is a raw expression of "is-ness"—of present moment awareness and being. In other words, the breath [read: *breadth*] of *blues haiku* is a keeping alive Black folks. Afrofuturism. It is "an acceptance of pain, humor, beauty and non-beauty, death and rebirth, surprise and life. Always life."[102]

But isn't all Black poetry?

I am a self-taught poet. However, I consider my television encounter with Maya Angelou the impetus of a formal poetic study. After watching her deliver "On the Pulse of Morning," I spent the remainder of my 7th grade year reading her autobiographies. I was so enamored by Angelou's story, my mother—a former elementary school teacher who integrated the all-white school in which she would spend thirty years teaching third graders—took me to an Angelou lecture. I was in 8th grade by then, no more than 13 years old, and, besides family reunions and Sunday school services, there was nothing more life-giving than watching and listening to Angelou juxtapose her life story with poetry—as well as music and dance:

Mari Evans's "Who Can Be Born Black."
Langston Hughes's "Mother to Son."
William Shakespeare's "My Mistress' Eyes."
Paul Laurence Dunbar's "Little Brown Baby."

According to Angelou, who recited Dunbar's 1895 "A Negro Love Song" while snapping her fingers and tapping her feet, "Love Song" was the first rap, which made Dunbar the first rapper—84 years before Sugar Hill. A sugared hill. That's what Black poems are. Sugared hills. Stories of an acclivous life sweetened through Black folks' expressions of joy, creativity, love, and triumph.

In one breath, Paul Laurence Dunbar is writing poems about Black folks wearing masks that grin and lie, and in another he's shuckin an' jivin about seein' his lady home last night. *The tom-tom cries and the tom-tom laughs*. Certainly, there's nothing new under this American sun; just new ways of making them felt. New ways of expressing a Black life unexpected to survive America's attempt at annihilation.

being[103]

I prefer no name
for I am everything
& nothing at all
can contain the wonderment
of my being All

that I am & not
born into a bodied text
read & redefined
thru sets of cultural norms
perceiving me as certain

I prefer no name
void of interpretations
where meanings collapse
into moments of crisis
suspending me in between:

up, down, sidebyside
there, nowhere, everywhere
fluid as water
stretching rules of existence
until I'm recognized, *free*

tanka for Anna Julia Cooper, Pauli Murray, & Mary Church Terrell[104]

intellectual:
Black women claiming head space
inside a text space
dominated by white space
creating space for Black thought

representation & controlling images[105]

no mammy nor mule
has controlled my images
more than white Jesus
looming over pastor's head
—the everlasting savior

haiku narrative: coming (inside) out[106]

I.
coming inside out
I shatter the glass closet
surveilling my sex

I am visible
to a necropolitic
aiming to kill me—

my woman's body
fodder for big game hunters
obsessed w/my skin

II.
Black faces wear masks[107]
muting the threat of violence
inciting white rage[108]

tanka: centering prison abolition[109]

unmake public schools
methodically defunded
to expand prisons
incarcerating Black folks
thru hidden curriculums

tanka: coming out

if Black folk came out
the world will look upon them
& be so ashamed[110]
it'd offer its depraved face:
white. w/horns & serpent tongue

tanka: erotic chaos[111]

enter inside me
in all my broken pieces—
my fragmented pores
wide open to receiving
radical transformation

haiku narrative for the Indigenous[112]

refuse the ruses
of U.S. citizenship
& treaty making

don't offer consent
nor ur belonging w/in
a settler system

focused on whiteness
as a necropolitic
choking ur power

you!—ur own best thing[113]—
reclaim ur sovereignty
& refuse to die!

tanka: werk it![114]

shake it, don't break it![115]
repurpose & remake it!
an economy
of trans protest performance /
self-possessing Black power

for my trans people[116]: a tanka narrative[117]

between slavery
& colonialism
lies liberal thought
intimately connecting
four continents of people—

Black & brown people
"saved" by liberal projects
of civility
reserved for white settling men
who name themselves *all-knowing*

master of no one
idea about the other
whose traded bodies
ploughed a bourgeoisie europe
on which new worlds were ordered

thinking of Toni Morrison & Gloria Anzaldúa[118]: a tanka

this bridge called my back
a sacred text men traverse[119]
—a kind of hot thing[120]
on which they capitalize
& decry women's genius

concentration camps: a tanka[121]

fvk America
& its democratic ruse
to garner consent
by pinkwashing[122] its polis
into solidarity

"me/we"[123]: tanka narrative for Frantz Fanon, Achille Mbembe, Angela Y. Davis, Ann duCille, C. Riley Snorton, Treva Ellison, Hortense Spillers, Tiffany King, Audra Simpson, Summer Kim Lee, & Lisa Lowe

the fact of Blackness[124]
exists in its Negritude[125]
& audacity
to counter necropower[126]
w/Black love & resilience

we in glass closets
wear the mask that grins & lies[127]
inside prison walls[128]
we rewritin grammar books[129]
as sacred as our bodies

from the inside out
we refuse grand narratives
denying our truths
spread across four continents
like the holy ghost werks it

after reading adrienne maree brown's "Emergent Strategies"[130]

we inch wide mile deep
into a (r)evolution
like dandelions
taking root in barren fields
waiting for lion toothed leaves

We. Dandelions
with Gwendolyn Brooks in mind [131]

We.   Black folks rooted like dandelions
          in deserted fields, backyards, & concrete
We.   reach sunlight in our reach for Zion
          pushing thru rain & unbearable heat
We.   emerge slightly scathed, tho deeply sowed
          steadfast like Daniel in the lion's den
We.   Shadrach, Meshach, & Abednego
          w/a mother's nature of New World wrens
We.   sing freedom songs crescendoing loud
          abovesoundabovesound surpassing sound
We.   still die too soon, but the soil's been ploughed
          for more dandelions to push thru ground
We.   break new earth into a paradise
We.   seed in them & they keep us alive

a minor figure[132]: a tanka

I beach on the roof[133]
top bare/ly realizing
flashing ain't storm proof
against white camera men
ensuring torrential rains

**tanka for the Mattie Crawfords[134] & the Esther Browns[135]
(or the anatomy of Negro crime poem)**

> they hit the dance floor
> trippin the light fantastic
> into the sho nuff
> of Black radicalism
> as sultry as a slow drag

tanka for Frances Ellen Watkins Harper & 'em

when the country births
a race of freed Black women
it will know itself
as one nation under God
baptized in democracy

when (Black) women won the right to vote: her/story unfinished[136]

no. 1: 1870

I'da be well[137] when—
white folks get off their high horse
reigns held by klansmen
suckling still their mother's breast
home to flawed democracy

no. 2: 1920

I'da be well if—
all white women suffragists
joined the Black movement
ensuring citizenship
rights they implore for themselves

no. 3: 1965

I'da be well but—
Black women won voting rights
uniting the states
in a *temporary* act
of multiracial democracy

no. 4: 2017

I'da be well 'cept—
white women voted in trump
post Obama's reign
reawakening the nation
to the 1870s

on DuBois & his *Philadelphia Report*[138]

Truth comes before Kings
convinced that humanity
can be found in facts
retrieved in social reports
engineered by the other

Black book: a tanka narrative

white folks misread us
like a book they've tried to ban
from school libraries—
li(v)es buried in narratives
of categorized white lies

meant to tear at us
like ripping out the pages
splintering the spine
of a book so sagacious
it's incomprehensible

can't be understood
except by our permission[139]
which they often steal
but not like bibliophiles
or book thieves loving language

but colonizers
whose american grammar
calls us out our names
thru syntax that thingifies
our human composition

tanka for the Combahee River Collective[140]: wayward women

Jesus ain't white / like
Black radical tradition
be more than Black men
leading movements cementing
anarchy in their likeness

tanka narrative for the LA feminist who demonstrated a pelvic exam at the local bookstore[141]

you opened ur legs
in that feminist bookstore
like we open books
probing pages for gospels
sweeter than Amazing Grace

ur body's a poem—
a vagina monologue
we can't stop reading
ur story is our own
comingtobeing Lilith[142]—

we know ourselves
as we're known by Creator
orchestrating life
force/d in our womanhood
too deep for theology

outside the domain[143]

outside the domain—

> we are dinosaurs
> w/no logic nor language—
> prehistoric folk
> needing to be colonized
> in european knowledge
>
> a grammar of greed
> as epistemologies
> structuring hate speech
> rhetorically composed
> as reason for larceny
>
> we—stripped of selfhood
> transposed in Jurassic Parks
> for their amusement
> & scientific research
> masking their narcissisms
>
> unbeknownst to them
> we are the divine other
> w/unscathed spirits
> who turned ourselves into ourselves[144]
>
> we ain't dinosaurs.
> we gods.

Braiding Sweetgrass[145] pomes

1. a citizenship guide

>from fields to prisons
>Black life be a whole service
>of ecosystems
>planted inside fixed structures
>to make white life possible

2. the honorable harvest pome

>she was a wild thing
>shimmering at the lake's edge
>standing in a blaze
>of photosynthesis
>sweet as Shug Avery's kisses

3. windigo footprints poem

>white man windigo
>lost his soul to gain the world[146]—
>which still ain't enuf
>so he colonizes space
>fixing his gaze on the moon[147]

4. people of corn, people of light (proclamation)

>for western science
>to see plants as its teacher
>it'd, too, have to see
>Black folks as human beings
>beyond objectivity

5. collateral damage poem

if amphibians
are the most vulnerable
they must be Black girls
unable to breathe clean air
sullied by man's appetite

who will rescue her
& attest her right to be—
known as she is known
to live in her sovereignty
free from man's penetration?

from sea to shining see: a tanka narrative[148]

to see from below—
to see from submerged viewpoints
the space of vision
that surrounds & passes thru—
illuminates Black bodies

we, like anglerfish,
live w/in ecologies
an unfolding source
of natural elements
swimming in murky waters

no. we did not drown
when thrown overboard to sea;
we breathed the water
& birthed aquatic babies
never needing air to live

in/tangible space
of emergence where rivers
move into the flow & muck
of Black life unexpected

to survive / to know
rivers ancient as the world
& older than blood
flowing warm in human veins[149]—
to know the world as it was

before extraction
of dams & mines & bodies
belonging elsewhere
splitting nature & culture
until we strangely exist

NOTES

[1] See full essay collected in Amiri Baraka's *SOS: Poems 1961-2013*, edited by Paul Vangelisti, Grover Press, 2014, pp. 597-599.

[2] See full essay in Audre Lorde's *Sister Outsider: Essays and Speeches*, Crossing Press, 1984, pp. 36-39.

[3] Essay first published in *Cultural Critique*, no. 6, Spring 1987. It is also collected in *Within the Circle: An Anthology of African American Literary Criticism from the Harlem Renaissance to the Present*, edited by Angelyn Mitchell, Duke University Press, 1994, pp. 348-359.

[4] See full essay/poem in June Jordan's *On Call: Political Essays*, South End Press, 1985, pp. 87-98.

[5] See Lucille Clifton's "surely i am able to write poems," collected in *Mercy*, BOA Editions, 2004, p. 23.

[6] See Amiri Baraka's 1966 "SOS" poem reprinted in the front matter of *SOS Poems 1961-2013*.

[7] See June Jordan's 1974 "Calling on All Silent Minorities" included in *New Days: Poems of Exile and Return* and reprinted in *Directed by Desire*, p. 149. Inarguably, Jordan's poem is a response to Baraka's "SOS."

[8] According to Yoruba religion, the Òrìṣàs are the spirits sent by Ọlọrun, the Almighty, to guide humanity in right living.

[9] Ògún is the traditional deity of warriors and spirit of metal work.

[10] Ṣàngó, known for his anger, is a spirit of thunder, lightning, and justice.

[11] Aganju, described as Ṣàngó's father or brother, is a warrior who fights by shooting fire.

[12] Ọṣun is the goddess of divinity, femininity, fertility, beauty, and love.

[13] Ọlọrun is the Almighty, who sends the Òrìṣàs to guide humanity in right living.

[14] Àṣẹ is a West African philosophical concept through which existence is made possible; it is spiritual energy given to empower living things so they can live rightly.

[15] Title is taken from Maya Angelou's 2002 autobiography, *A Song Flung Up to Heaven*, the sixth of her seven-part series.

[16] Text taken from Dolores Kendrick's 1989 "Sidney, Looking for Her Mother . . . ," third stanza, lines 34-35. Full poem is anthologized in

In Search of Color Everywhere: A Collection of African American Poetry, edited by E. Ethelbert Miller, Stewart, Tabori, & Chang, 1994, pp. 25-27.

[17] Text taken from Mari Evans's 1979 "Who Can Be Born Black," second stanza, 6th line. Although this poem is included in Evans's *I am a Black Woman: Poems by Mari Evans*, 1964, the full poem is anthologized in *In Search of Color Everywhere*, p. 62.

[18] Text taken from Langston Hughes's 1926 "The Negro Speaks of Rivers," third stanza, second line. Full poem is included in Hughes's *The Weary Blues*, which is reprinted in *The Collected Poems of Langston Hughes*, edited by Arnold Rampersad, Alfred A. Knopf, 2000, p. 23.

[19] April 2014, the Boko Haram, an Islamic terrorist group, kidnapped 276 female students who were in Nigeria's Government Girls Secondary School taking a final examination. As of April 2021, over 100 of the girls remain missing.

[20] Also known as Amina Queen of Zazzau, who ruled and expanded Zazzau territory (now the city of Zaria in the north-west region of Nigeria) in the mid-16th century.

[21] In George S. Schuyler's 1926 essay, "The Negro Art Hokum," he claimed Negro art nonsense and likened the Negro experience to that of White Americans—so calling Blacks, "lampblacked Anglo-Saxons." Schuyler's essay is collected in *The Wiley Blackwell Anthology of African American Literature, Vol. 2: 1920 to the Present*, edited by Gene Andrew Jarrett, 2014, pp. 221-222.

[22] Reference from Langston Hughes's 1926 essay, "The Negro Artist and the Racial Mountain," which is a response to Schuyler's abovementioned essay. Hughes's essay is also collected in *The Wiley Blackwell Anthology*, pp. 210-212.

[23] According to W.E.B. DuBois's 1926 essay, "The Criteria of Negro Art," for art to be beautiful, it must be grounded in Truth and goodness. DuBois's essay is collected in *The Wiley Blackwell Anthology*, pp. 157-163.

[24] Reference to Kehinde Wiley's 2018 portrait of Barack Obama, which is housed in the Smithsonian's National Portrait Gallery, Washington, DC.

[25] Title taken from and poem inspired by Sue Monk Kidd's 1996 memoir, *Dance of the Dissident Daughter*, about her journey from Christian religiosity to the divine feminine.

[26] Eric Garner died in Staten Island, NY 2014 after police officer

Daniel Pantaleo placed him in a chokehold. Although Garner was heard telling officers 11 times he couldn't breathe, Pantaleo maintained his choke hold. When he did release Garner, Pantaleo pushed Garner's face into the sidewalk. Medics arrived on the scene seven minutes later, during which time, Garner lay on the sidewalk motionless. According to reports, EMT did not give Garner oxygen nor did they administer medical aide. Pantaleo was not indicted for Garner's murder; however, in 2019, a judge overseeing an NYPD disciplinary hearing regarding Garner's death recommended Pantaleo be fired. "I can't breathe," like Michael Brown's "Hands up, Don't shoot," became protestors' chilling chant in marches that ensued across the nation.

[27] Sandra Bland, 28, was found hanged in a Waller County, Texas jail cell three days after she was arrested for a minor traffic violation July 2015. Arresting officer, Brian Encinia, thirsty for an arrest, rushed Bland, who switched lanes to let him pass. Because Bland "failed to signal," Encinia pulled her over, eventually pulling her out of her car and arresting her. Brian Encinia was not brought up on any charges, but he was terminated by the Texas Department of Public Safety.

[28] In August 1831, enslaved African American preacher Nat Turner led a slave revolt in South Hampton County, Virginia that killed at least 51 white people. According to Turner, the revolt was divinely ordained.

[29] donald trump threatened protestors with "vicious dogs and ominous weapons" during the 2020 riots (read: *protests*) resulting from George Floyd's murder. However, at the time this sonnet was written in 2016, trump was on the presidential campaign and referred to Black neighborhoods as ghettos, promising to eradicate "the problems" of the inner city, which he also compared to war zones.

[30] This line, along with the third, directly responds to Claude McKay's 1919 sonnet, "If We Must Die." The first line of his sonnet reads: "If we must die, let it not be like hogs"; and the last two lines read: "Like men we'll face the murderous, cowardly pack, / Pressed to the wall, dying, but fighting back!" McKay's poem was written in response to America's "Red Summer," during which 25 or so race riots and resulting fatalities swept across the nation. McKay's sonnet is collected in *In Search of Color Everywhere*, p. 37.

[31] "If the people could fly" references Virginia Hamilton's 1985 *The People Could Fly: American Black Folktales*. The reoccurring line also

refers to the myth of the flying Africans who fled slavery by lifting their bodies and flying back home. Toni Morrison's 1977 *Song of Solomon* also reflects the flying African myth.

[32] This line direclty responds to Paul Laurence Dunbar's 1899 "Sympathy" poem, which inspired the title of Maya Angelou's 1969 autobiography, *I Know Why the Caged Bird Sings*. The second line in Dunbar's third stanza reads: "I know why the caged bird sings, ah me, / When his wing is bruised and his bosom sore,—" Dunbar's poem is collected in *The Collected Poetry of Paul Laurence Dunbar*, edited by Joanne M. Braxton, University of Virginia Press, 1993, p. 314.

[33] At the time of this writing, an extensive list of Black women lynched in America was available at http://theblacklistpub.ning.com/forum/topics/lynching-victims-blackwomen. However, that source is no longer available. Nonetheless, David B. Baker and Gilbert Garcia's 2019 "An Analytical History of Black Female Lynchings in the U.S., 1838-1969" is worth reading. It can be accessed at: https://www.qualitativecriminology.com.

[34] Accused of murder; lynched in Hernando, MS, 1878.

[35] Lynched in Clayton, GA, 1880.

[36] At age 35, accused of arson; lynched in Newberry, SC, 1881.

[37] Accused of murder; lynched in Madison, TN, 1887.

[38] Accused of murder; lynched in Chatham, NC, 1885.

[39] Accused of murder; lynched in Tattnall, GA, 1886.

[40] Accused of theft; lynched in W. Carroll, LA, 1887.

[41] Accused of arson; lynched in Henry, AL, 1891.

[42] Lynched in Centerville, AL, 1981.

[43] Accused of poisoning a well; lynched in Jackson, MS, 1893.

[44] Accused of arson; lynched in Lynchburg, VA, 1893.

[45] Lynched in Trigg County, KY, 1895.

[46] Lynched in Scottsville, KY, 1894.

[47] Lynched in New Orleans, LA, 1895.

[48] Accused of poisoning; lynched in Baton Rouge, LA, 1895.

[49] Accused of stealing a Bible; lynched in Colleton, SC, 1895.

[50] Accused of arson; lynched in Carrolton, AL, 1893.

[51] Accused of murder; lynched in Jefferson, AL, 1897.

[52] Accused of race prejudice; lynched in Williamsburg, SC, 1898.

[53] Accused of race prejudice; lynched in Hickory Plains, AK, 1900.

[54] Accused of having bootlegging parents; lynched—with her sister, Eula—in Jasper County, GA, 1915.

[55] Accused of miscegenation and living with her white husband; lynched in Jefferson, LA, 1896.

[56] Accused of murder; lynched in Pinehurst, GA, 1912.

[57] Accused of murder; lynched in Greenville, AL, 1895.

[58] Accused of murder; lynched in Troy, SC, 1902.

[59] Husband accused of murder; lynched in Mitchell, GA, 1906.

[60] Accused of murder; lynched in Okemah, OK, 1911.

[61] Accused of aiding in escape; lynched in Newberry, FL, 1916.

[62] Accused of murder; lynched in Douglass, GA, 1920.

[63] Accused of having prior knowledge of murder; lynched—with her mother, Betsey—in Carrolton, MS, 1901.

[64] See Alice Walker's *Hard Times Require Furious Dancing: New Poems*, New World Library, 2010.

[65] From Hughes's "The Negro Artist and the Racial Mountain," anthologized in *Within the Circle*, pp. 55-59.

[66] See Larry Neal's 1968 essay, "The Black Arts Movement," first published in *TDR: The Drama Review* 12.4 and reprinted in *SOS—Calling All Black People: A Black Arts Movement Reader*, edited by John H. Bracey, Jr., Sonia Sanchez, and James Smethurst, University of Massachusetts Press, 2014, pp. 55-66.

[67] Definition retrieved from *Wikipedia*, "Hip-Hop Music," 2 October 2023.

[68] Line from Heron's 1970 *Whitey's on the Moon*, recorded on his *Small Talk at 125th and Lenox* album.

[69] Line from Amiri Baraka's 1969 "Black Art," first published in *Black Magic*, and reprinted in *SOS*, pp. 149-150.

[70] Line from Nikki Giovanni's 1969 "Ego Tripping (there must be a reason why)."

[71] Line from Mari Evans's "Who Can Be Born Black" poem.

[72] Line from Countee Cullen's 1925 "Incident" poem, first published in *Color* and collected in *My Soul's High Song: The Collected Writings of Countee Cullen*, edited by Gerald Early, Anchor Books, 1991, p. 90.

[73] Line from Zora Neale Hurston's 1937 *Their Eyes Were Watching God* novel.

[74] This line, and the previous, taken from Claude McKay's 1919 sonnet "If We Must Die," reprinted in *In Search of Color Everywhere*, p. 37.

[75] This line, and previous, taken from Langston Hughes' 1925 "I, Too," reprinted in *The Collected Poems*, p. 46.

[76] Title of Public Enemy's 1989 rap song.

[77] 1980 song and EP title from N.W.A.

[78] Title of Queen Latifah's 1989 rap song.

[79] Title of Body Count's (featuring Ice T) 1992 rap song.

[80] Title of KRS-One's 1988 single from his Stop the Violence Movement.

[81] Title ("Action") of Buju Banton's 1997 reggae song.

[82] See Maya Angelou's 1993 Presidential Inauguration poem, "On the Pulse of Morning," collected in *Maya Angelou: The Complete Poetry*, Random House, 2015, pp. 261-266.

[83] See Audre Lorde's 1978 poem, "Hanging Fire," first printed in *The Black Unicorn* and collected in *The Collected Poems of Audre Lorde*, W.W. Norton & Company, 1997, p. 308.

[84] Title of Nikki Giovanni's, 1968 poem, "Ego Tripping (*there may be a reason why*)," first printed in *Re: Creation* and reproduced in *The Collected Poetry of Nikki Giovanni 1968-1998*, William Morrow, 2003, pp. 125-126.

[85] Lines from Mari Evans' 1964 poem, "Who Can Be Born Black?"

[86] Title and line from Gwendolyn Brooks' 1963 poem, "We Real Cool," first printed in *The Bean Eaters* and reproduced in *Blacks*, Third World Press, 1987, p. 331.

[87] Title of Maya Angelou's 1978 poem, "Phenomenal Woman," included in *And Still I Rise*, Random House, 1978, and reprinted in *The Complete Poetry*, Random House, 2015, pp. 126-127.

[88] Line from Mari Evans' 1970 poem, "I Am a Black Woman."

[89] See Alice Walker's *In Search of Our Mothers' Gardens: Womanist Prose*, Harcourt Brace Jovanovich, 1983.

[90] Lines from Ntozake Shange's 1975 choreopoem, *For Colored Girls Who Have Considered Suicide / When the Rainbow is Enuf.*

[91] Title of Beverly Guy-Sheftall's anthology, *Words of Fire: An Anthology of African American Feminist Thought*, The New Press, 1995.

[92] Title of Sonia Sanchez's 1987 poetry collection, *Under a Soprano Sky,* Africa World Press.

[93] Title of Pat Parker's 1978 poetry collection first published by Diana Press, as well as a refrain in "Movement in Black" poem.

[94] Lines from Margaret Walker's 1942 poem, "For My People," collected in *In Search of Color Everywhere*, pp. 57-58.

[95] Line from Lucille Clifton's "my poem," printed in *an ordinary woman*, 1974, and collected in *good woman: poems and a memoir 1969-1980*, BOA Editions, 1987, p. 144.

96 Line from June Jordan's 1978 "Poem for South African Women," printed in *Passion*, 1980, collected in *Directed by Desire*, published by Copper Canyon Press, p. 278.

97 A nod to Valerie Boyd's *Wrapped in Rainbows: The Life of Zora Neale Hurston*, Scribner, 2003.

98 King's 1958 essay, "An Experiment in Love," was first published in his *Stride Toward Freedom: The Montgomery Circle*. In it, King discusses "agape love" as a radical practice that can restore community.

99 See Jerry W. Ward Jr.'s "Introduction" in his 1997 *Trouble the Water: 250 Years of African-American Poetry*, The Penguin Group, pp. xix-xxiv.

100 See Audre Lorde's 1977 "Poetry Is Not a Luxury" essay—written two years after BAM's decline and three years into the Hip-Hop Movement. It is collected in her *Sister Outsider*, 1984.

101 See full interview, titled "Sonia Sanchez: The Power of the Word: A Love Haiku," at pbs.org.

102 See Sanchez's 2021 "haikuography," in *Sonia Sanchez: Collected Poems*, Beacon Press, 2021, pp. 363-364.

103 In Chapter One: "Becoming the Loon" of Stacey Waite's 2017 *Teaching Queer: Radical Possibilities for Writing and Knowing*, Waite suggests an unknowing of all things known, including how one knows oneself. She argues to unknow the self leads to an uninhibited imagination where one is always *becoming*—one is always being, never stuck in or to an identity that doesn't belong to her or him.

104 Anna Julia Cooper, Pauli Murray, and Mary Church Terrell were Black women theorists; they were intellectual race women, says Brittney C. Cooper in her 2017 *Beyond Respectability: The Intellectual Thought of Race Women*, whose commitment to social justice, specifically race and gender matters, positioned them as "models of racial leadership and public lecturing . . . [thus] creat[ing] the paradigms for contemporary modes of Black public intellectual engagement" (p. 15).

105 "Mammies, Matriarchs, and Other Controlling Images," the fourth chapter of Patricia Hill Collins' 1990 *Black Feminist Thought: Knowledge, Consciousness, and the Politics of Empowerment*, inspired this poem, along with my childhood memories of sitting in the church's sanctuary and seeing, above the pulpit, a mural of a barely naked white, blue-eyed, blonde-haired Jesus floating in the

clouds, surrounded by white rose-cheeked cherubs.

[106] In his 2014 article response to both Richard Iton and the symptomatic question: "Who's Out in Hip Hop," C. Riley Snorton proposes Eve Sedgwick's *glass closet* as metaphor to explore "how black gender and sexuality is subject to hypervisibility and confinement, spectacle and speculation in which anti-blackness and the pornotrope logics of visualizing blackness give rise to the glass closet as a collective rather than individual concern" (p. 285). In other words, Snorton writes about the see-thru boxes queer hip-hop artists (Azaelia Banks; Frank Ocean; Syd the Kyd; Lil B; and Nicki Minaj) are placed in that traps them inside other folks' judgments re: their gender and sexuality. These mass onlookers reduce Black hip-hop artists to their flesh and objectify them for their consumption, he explains, thus forcing them into creative ways of navigating such sexual publicity.

[107] In his 1895 poem, "We Wear the Mask," Paul Laurence Dunbar implies that Black faces/bodies who are made hyper visible, though confined (and ridiculed) by the oppressor's dehumanizing gaze, must "wear the mask that grins and lies; hides cheeks and shades eyes" (lines 1-2) with hope that "the explosive possibility of blackness is momentarily unseen," says Snorton (p. 299). In other words, if the oppressor can't read me, then s/he won't realize my scheming toward Black liberation; that moment of being unseen, therefore, serves as divine space where freedom is made more possible. "We Wear the Mask" is collected in *The Collected Poetry of Paul Laurence Dunbar*, edited by Joanne M. Braxton.

[108] "White rage" responds to Carol Anderson's 2016 *White Rage: The Unspoken Truth of Our Racial Divide* wherein Anderson unapologetically attributes the stall in civil rights movements and social justice, as well as the unconscionable violence inflicted upon Black bodies, to white folks enraged at the idea of Black citizenship and human rights.

[109] In her 2016 "Centering Prison Abolition in Women's Gender, and Sexuality Studies," Priya Kandaswamy argues an abolitionist pedagogy may liberate Women's, Gender, and Sexuality Studies (WGSS) programs from a neoliberalist curriculum that sustains the prison-industrial complex thereby maintaining the white supremacist, capitalist patriarchy. According to Kandaswamy, who explains how neoliberalism operates in WGSS programs via "safe spaces," service-learning projects, and identity politics, "Abolitionist

frameworks challenge us to *let go of our investments in the world the way it is*, making space instead to imagine what a world without violence might look like" [emphasis mine] (p. 10).

[110] Although Snorton's 2014 essay, to which this poem responds, is about queer/ed Blacks, I am thinking about the full throttle exposure of Black folks' spiritual genius that shames and frightens white people into believing Black folks are the Christ-like figures they've sent to the cross. When I read Langston Hughes' 1926 "I, Too" poem, particularly lines 16-17, wherein he says: "They'll see how beautiful I am / And be ashamed—" I imagine a spiritual awakening of white folks toward Black divinity.

[111] Using Audre Lorde's 1978 "Uses of the Erotic" and Julie Dash's 1991 *Daughters of the Dust* to ground her 2019 "Our Cherokee Uncles: Black and Native Erotics," Tiffany King examines the dangerously queered lovership between Dash's St. Julien Lastchild, a Native American, and Iona Peazant, an African American. King claims their choosing to love each other is a radical, abolitionist practice that invites decolonization and enables futurism, particularly for the Black person who has no future without the other's alliance. Because St. Julien Lastchild and Iona Peazant choose to love each other inside a system that has already marked them for death because they simply exist as Native and African, the two "opposing" lovers immediately activate abolitionist practice, for they become co-conspirators against a system designed to annihilate queered people.

[112] In her 2017 "The Ruse of Consent and the Anatomy of 'Refusal,'" Audra Simpson examines the Kahnawa'kehró:non's history of refusing consent and citizenship of U.S. settler states by refusing to assimilate to American cultures by holding on to the truth of who they are. In other words, Simpson argues that Native American agency and authenticity counters American imperialism.

[113] In Toni Morrison's 1987 *Beloved*, Paul D tells Sethe: "You your best thing, Sethe. You are" (p. 273). Sethe, who killed her daughter Beloved, believed Beloved was her best thing.

[114] In their 2017 "The Labor of Werqing It," Treva Ellison examines the protest and performance strategies of LA-based Black femme performer, Sir Lady Java, arguing that drag was a labored werk in resistance. According to Ellison, Java, a trans performer during the 1960s, werked against and w/in regular harassment by the LAPD. As such, says Ellison, Java's labored visibility was a political tool by

which she challenged gender norms, anti-Blackness, criminalization of sex work, and capitalism.
[115] In the 8th verse of their controversial, misogynistic 1991 "Pop That Coochie," The 2 Live Crew shout: "Shake it! Don't break it! / It took your momma nine months to make it / Bend over and spread 'em, girl / Show-w-w me those pussy pearls," which feels like an appropriate first line for a poem intended to flip the script, wherein "werking it" is not attributed to only those born with female genitalia. As a Miami native born in the late 70s, I am well acquainted w/The 2 Live Crew whose misogynistic language so objectified women and offended respectable Black folks, their music was (almost) banned in America. However, the U.S. Supreme Court refused to proceed with the censorship case brought upon them in 1994, thus marking The 2 Live Crew leaders in rap musicians' right to free speech.
[116] Although *trans* is most associated with the transsexual community, I am extending trans, first, to Black folks, whose transport through the transatlantic slave trade culminated in the African Diaspora; and second, to the forced migration of brown folks.
[117] In the first chapter of her 2015 *The Intimacies of Four Continents*, Lisa Lowe provides a "genealogy of modern liberalism" (p. 3) by examining the promises, divisions, and conditions of a liberalist project created to benefit the European colonizer. According to Lowe, little is known about the intimate relationships amongst 18-19th century European settlers, Indigenous peoples, as well as Africans and Asians in America's "new world" despite the research already produced re: trade and migration. Much of our failure to know, explains Lowe, has to do with the academy's disciplining, naturalized forgetting, and liberal ways of understanding. Lowe insists that people do away w/traditional reading and researching practices that insist upon a knowing that sustains settler colonialism and, therefore, the oppression of Black and brown folks—the very people who created the conditions for liberty but are not allowed it.
[118] Chicana feminist scholar, who, along w/Cherríe Moraga, edited (1981) *This Bridge Called My Back: Writings by Radical Women of Color*. More specifically, the anthology includes a collection of essays, narratives, poems, and artwork reflecting the experiences of Black and brown women in a feminist movement that privileged whiteness. *This Bridge* has often been contributed to the

development of Third World Feminism and, undoubtedly, grounds intersectionality theory and research.

[119] In her brazen-faced essay, "The Occult of True Black Womanhood" (1994), Ann duCille asserts that "the occult of true black womanhood" is being blasphemed by the other (white man, woman, and black man) who has taken up interest in her body and subject matter because, basically, it's the new flavor of the year. Her essay, which oscillates between inquiry and emphatic statements, criticizes these onlookers—"*scopophiliacs*"—while acknowledging Black women writers who've been theorizing Black womanhood before it was an acknowledged "field of study."

[120] In *Beloved*'s chapter 22, Morrison's Beloved repeats the phrase "a hot thing" ten times as she remembers her voyage through the Middle Passage (pp. 210-213). While there are several interpretations of Morrison's "hot thing," I read the phrase as Beloved naming the love, passion, and desire she has for her mother, Sethe. That energy, and the relationship conjured from it, is a "hot thing" for which Beloved has no other name. I borrow Morrison's "hot thing," for it is a phrase that names what I believe is an incomprehensible, though enticing, energy, which is why men appropriate and commodify Black woman's genius.

[121] By mapping (from Canada to America to Israel) the media response toward the 2007 murder of Aqsa Parvez, a 16-year-old Islamic woman killed by her brother and father, Dana M. Olwan's "Pinkwashing the 'Honor Crime'" examines the right-wing activism honor crimes generate. Although *pinkwashing* is often associated with political (and marketing) practices used to dupe the LGBTQ community, Olwan relates pinkwashing to honor killing, for both are considered exceptional practices that justify the murdering and/or subjugation of another.

[122] Although *pinkwashing* is associated with tricking the LGBTQ community into consent, I am using it here as a synonym for *whitewashing*.

[123] Although hip-hop rap originated in 1973, Muhammad Ali, considered the greatest boxer of all time, was, undoubtedly, one of the first rappers (after Dunbar). He rhymed his way through interviews and speeches, coining the shortest poem, "Me, We." during his 1975 Harvard Commencement Address. His political and religious stance also situated him as a civil rights activist who refused to fight in the Vietnam War.

[124] Title of Fanon's chapter five essay, "The Fact of Blackness," from his 1967 *Black Skin White Masks*. In this essay, Fanon examines the ontology of the Black person, who seemingly exists in negation to white folks. Oh! But *Negritude*!

[125] *Negritude* is a movement or concept propelled by francophone intellectuals, writers, and politicians, namely, Léopold Senghor and Aimé Césaire. It affirmed the value of Black ontology through Black culture—like America's 1920s Harlem Renaissance.

[126] In Achille Mbembe's 2003 "Necropolitics," translated by Libby Meintjes, Mbembe conceptualizes necropolitics—the power (also defined as "sovereignty" or "politics") of death. By examining the interrelationship of terror, death, and freedom, Mbembe historicizes the political violence of Germany's Holocaust, America's slavery, Africa's apartheid, and the current Palestinian occupation by Israel. Throughout his essay, Mbembe illustrates how necropolitics operate and evolve: from "the serialization of technical mechanisms for putting people to death" (p. 18); to the "tension between the public's passion for blood and notions of justice and revenge" (pp. 18-19); to "expulsion from humanity" (p. 21); "colonial appropriation"; (p. 23) and the creation of "war machines" (p. 30).

[127] First line in Paul Laurence Dubar's "We Wear the Mask" poem.

[128] Reference to mass incarceration of Black folks but specifically to Angela Davis's 2003 "Political Prisoners, Prisons, and Black Liberation." In it, Davis defines and discusses the political prisoner and the working class as conduits for Black liberation. She begins her essay discussing state sanctioned violence as evidenced by the police's common promise to "maintain law and order," which really means maintain the mass murder and subjection of Black and brown people. In her opening paragraphs, Davis hints at neoliberalism as well as Gramsci's notions re: *coercion* and *consent* and Karl Marx's *superstructures,* like prison systems, through which the ruling class White American maintains his capitalist endeavors, which are always racist. As such, she explains, the prisons and penal systems are racist superstructures that coerce its victims and targets, while terrorizing minoritized communities through forced guilty pleas, extended sentences, abuse, and murder. Like Mbembe, Angela Davis's essay critiques the dominant political power's right to kill through false convictions, unjust penal systems, and mass incarcerations meant to maintain the working class's obedience.

[129] This phrase references Hortense Spillers's 1987 "Mama's Baby,

90

Papa's Maybe: An American Grammar Book," her seminal essay wherein she rhetorically excavates America's slavery archive, while explicating its linguistic terrorism, in order to disrupt the meta narrative whose white American scribers have semantically mis/named, defined, and dehumanized the enslaved African and, thus, the African-American family. She argues, therefore, that "the project of liberation for African-Americans . . . [is] to break apart, to rupture violently the laws of American behavior that make such *syntax* possible; [and] to introduce a new *semantic* field/fold more appropriate to his/her own historic movement" [author's emphasis] (p. 16). Spillers grounds her four-part discussion on Daniel Patrick Moynihan's 1960s report re: the Black family. In it, he vilifies the Black working (and single) woman, blaming her for the absence of a father head. Moynihan claims, explains Spillers, that the matriarchal structure of the "Negro community . . . is so far out of line with the *rest of American society*, [thus] seriously retard[ing] the progress of the group as a whole, and impos[ing] a crushing burden on the Negro male" [author's emphasis] (p. 65). However, counters Spillers, American culture is out of line with most cultures wherein the female line determines a child's identity, not the patriarchal. But because in America the patriarchal line determines a child's identity, the Black family, particularly the mother, has been mis/named, misunderstood, and ill-regarded as has been the father whose relationship to his daughters has been fragmented.

[130] In her 2017 *Emergent Strategy: Shaping Change, Changing Worlds*, adrienne maree brown collects essays, poems, speeches, and spells that revel in the universe's magic—like the miracle in a specie's ability to sustain and grow itself by being itself and allowing other species the same freedom. According to brown, when a species, like the dandelion, is allowed to be itself, it inevitably forges mutual relationships that strengthen it as well as the community/ecosystem in which it thrives.

[131] In her 1963 "We Real Cool" poem, Gwendolyn Brooks, the first Black person to win the Pulitzer Prize (for her 1949 *Annie Allen*), ends each of her stanzas with an enjambment "we."

[132] Title borrowed from chapter two of Saidiyah Hartman's 2019 *Wayward Lives, Beautiful Experiments: Intimate Histories of Riotous Black Girls, Troublesome Women, and Queer Radicals*. "A Minor Figure" is framed w/in an image of a little Black girl posing nude on a couch. Her archived image, according to Hartman, is tagged:

"Trapped in an attic studio in Philadelphia, year 1882." However, although "A Minor Figure" is framed w/in that particular image— which illustrates the dehumanizing behavior of white folks who gazed upon and objectified Black girls' bodies—"A Minor Figure" also points toward Black girls, women, and radicals as marginalized *minor* figures who engaged in obscene practices as survival exercises.

[133] According to Hartman, "They (white folks who surveilled Blacks and photographed their dwellings) didn't know that the foyer, the fire escape, and the rooftop were a stretch of urban beach, not until the rich adopted the practice and sleeping on rooftops became fashionable" (*Wayward Lives*, 2019, p. 22).

[134] Talitha LeFlouria frames her 2015 *Chained in Silence: Black Women and Convict Labor in the New South,* inside the narrative of Mattie Crawford, who, at 16-years-old, was convicted of killing her abusive stepfather and sentenced to a life of "heavy work" in Georgia's state penitentiary, 1896. While imprisoned, Smith worked as a blacksmith, wore men's clothing, and exercised a fortitude that earned her the "freedom" of being the prison camp's gatekeeper. She notoriously became known as America's only woman blacksmith whose work exceeded that of male blacksmiths. According to LeFlouria, incarcerated Black women like Mattie Smith were trapped in a convict leasing system that profited private investors who funded industrialism. Thus, imprisoned Black women were just as responsible for industrialism as the men who are most credited for it, she says.

[135] Esther Brown is one of Hartman's "wayward" Black girls who engaged in leisurely activities, thus exercising an act of resistance. She doesn't give a shit about Black folks' respectability politics nor white folks' status quo.

[136] Title borrowed from and poem inspired by Lisa Tetrault's 2021 "When Women Won the Right to Vote: A History Unfinished." In it, Tetrault refutes US citizens' "right" to vote by rhetorically explicating, via a legal lens, the Constitution's misleading language as written in the 15th (1870) and 19th (1920) amendments as well as the 1965 Voting Rights Act. According to Tetrault, "The 'right to vote,' as we imagine it—as the most fundamental and important right democratic citizens possess—does not actually exist in the US" (p. 181). Tetrault details the progression of US suffrage in three parts. She explains: 1. how the 15th amendment, with its omission of

"white" in voter criteria, granted Black men voting "rights," while failing to free them of tactics used to prohibit their casting ballots (p. 183); 2. how the 19th amendment permitted women's voting rights by requiring states to eliminate the word "male" in its voting criteria but failed to ensure states granted Black women the right; and 3. how the 1965 Voting Rights Act, a temporary federal legislation that prohibited states from implementing disenfranchising voting tactics like poll taxes and literacy exams, gave Black women the "right" to vote (pp. 192-194). However, in *Shelby County v. Holder* (2013), the Voting Rights Act was "gutted," reports Tetrault, and America revealed itself as a '"flawed democracy'" (p. 194).

[137] Ida B. Wells (b. 1862, Mississippi) was a human rights activist-journalist-educator widely known for documenting lynchings, which resulted in her 1895 *The Red Record*. Wells also actively participated in Black woman's suffrage. According to Tetrault, who retells the events of the 1913 National American Woman Suffrage Association's Parade—held the day before Woodrow Wilson's inauguration and organized by Alice Paul, who insisted Black women march to the back—Ida B. Wells refused Paul's request and integrated the white woman's parade via the Illinois delegation ("When Women," 2021, p. 188).

[138] In Hartman's *Wayward Lives*, she explores (exposes?) W.E.B. DuBois's early life and his sociology work, which required him (at 28-years-old) to gather statistical information on Philadelphia's Seventh Ward Black community and to create reports showcasing Black life post slavery. His "findings" resulted in his 1899 *The Philadelphia Negro*. According to Hartman, "Philadelphia had been a laboratory for the nation's experiment in racial democracy and the premier stage on which *the future after slavery* was enacted" [author's emphasis] (p. 85). Therefore, shortly after he graduated from Harvard, DuBois was hired to conduct a survey on the Seventh Ward where white folks blamed Black migrants for the political corruption and crime there. "Why are you studying us? Wouldn't it be better to study white folks, since they are the ones who need changing?" asked the 5,000 people Hartman says DuBois interviewed (p. 99). "They wondered," writes Hartman, "what Negro was earnest or naïve enough to believe that truth alone would change white people?" (p. 99). Five years after publishing his report, DuBois composed *The Souls of Black Folk* (1903) wherein he famously argues the problem of the 20th century is the problem of the color line.

[139] In the 7th stanza of Nikki Giovanni's 1968 "Ego Tripping (there must be a reason why)," she writes: "I am so perfect so divine so ethereal so surreal / I cannot be comprehended / except by my permission."

[140] The Combahee River Collective (CRC) (named after the 1863 Combahee River Raid, orchestrated by Harriet Tubman who led the 2nd South Carolina Infantry responsible for aiding 750 or so emancipated slaves) is a Black feminist group whose founders, Barbara and Beverly Smith as well as Demita Frazier, drafted a statement that extended a narrowed vision of Black feminism to include identity politics. Organizing between 1974 and 1980, this radical group of Black lesbian women aimed to liberate Black women via consciousness-raising around matters such as capitalism, reproductive labor, and sexuality. As a liberation movement organized and led by women, the CRC also addressed, thus countered, the oft male-dominated liberation movements that duplicated the patriarchy's sexist/gendered behaviors. Keeanga-Yamahtta Taylor's 2017 *How We Get Free: Black Feminism and the Combahee River Collective*, which includes the CRC's statement, is a worthwhile read that includes interviews with CRC founders. (Note: The Combahee River, located in South Carolina, is named after the Combahee tribe of Native Americans.)

[141] In her 2019 *To Live Here, You Have to Fight: How Women Led Appalachian Movements for Social Justice*, Jessica Wilkerson charts the community organizing of poor and working-class white Appalachian women and their movements toward welfare rights. In chapter five, "'The Best Care in History': Interdependence and the Community Health Movement," Wilkerson notes that some folks contribute a time when a Los Angeles feminist demonstrated a self-exam in a feminist bookstore to the development of the self-help movement (p. 143). Although Wilkerson centers white Appalachian women, I imagine that this provocative in the bookstore teaching woman is a bodacious Black woman.

[142] Lilith is thought to be the first woman, before Eve.

[143] In Chapter One: "Imperialism, History, Writing and Theory," from Linda Tuhiwai Smith's 1999 *Decolonizing Methodologies: Research and Indigenous Peoples*, Smith explicates the interconnectedness of imperialism, history, writing, and theory, arguing that history—written by economist, scientists, bureaucrats, and philosophers and fashioned through colonialist imperialism—is a binary-driven,

chronologically chartered single narrative that assumes totality, universality, factual progressive development, and self-actualization (pp. 74-77). Because colonial imperialist history is established on "otherness," only those considered human have a story, have a *history*, explains Smith; everyone else, therefore, is pre-historic—*before* history is written. What if we Black folks were pre-historic? Could our bones have left white people with insights re: how to live human?

[144] A nod to Nikki Giovanni's 1968 "Ego Tripping (there must be a reason why)".

[145] The five tankas collected here respond to Robin Wall Kimmerer's 2013 *Braiding Sweetgrass: Indigenous Wisdom, Scientific Knowledge, and the Teaching of Plants,* Milkweed Editions. As the title of her work suggests, *Braiding Sweetgrass* is a comingtogether—a braiding—of native and traditional knowledges that inform Kimmerer's relationship with spirit-nature and herself. Each of the tankas are titled after a chapter from Kimmerer's text.

[146] This line references James Baldwin and Nikki Giovanni's 1971 *SOUL!* interview. During it, Baldwin tells Giovanni that white folks lost their soul to gain the world.

[147] This line is a shout out to Gil Scot Heron's 1970 *Whitey's on the Moon,* recorded on his *Small Talk at 125th and Lenox* album.

[148] This poem responds to three works: Macarena Gómez-Barris' 2017 *The Extractive Zone,* Alexis Pauline Gumbs's 2020 *Undrowned: Black Feminist Lessons from Marine Mammals,* and Katherine McKittrick's 2021 *Dear Science and Other Stories.* In her introductory chapter, Gómez-Barris explains an encounter with a "visual poet" whose work and artistic practice revealed the "getting ovuh" spirit of sentient beings dispossessed and oppressed by extractive capitalism. According to Gómez-Barris, by analyzing "extractive zones"—*portable places where Indigenous land and life are made into*—one will realize what (or whom) emerges from the material changes to social and ecological life that capitalists (also colonialists and imperialists) impose upon its native beings (p. xvi). In other words, what moves at the margins? What or who is the rising phoenix? What survived but was meant to die? Who are these Jesus people? Similarly, Gumbs's *Undrowned* exposes the under/otherworld of creative survival. Likening marine mammals as the "other" upon whom dominating human beings impose their capitalist endeavors and desires, thus threatening marine life, Gumbs first reminds Black

folk that they, through their ancestors, can survive and breathe under water—under "unbreathable circumstances . . . in the chokehold of racial gendered ableist capitalism" (p. 2); and second, invites Black folk to evolve new ways of breathing, new ways of living as Black. Finally, McKittrick's *Dear Science*, specifically her third chapter, "The Smallest Cell Remembers a Sound," reveals liner notes from Drexciya's 1997 *The Quest* album (pp. 54-55). Their liner notes propose the possibility of humans, specifically pregnant Africans, breathing under water after being thrown overboard during the Middle Passage. McKittrick uses the band's liner notes, which she claims is a cosmogony, to illustrate how marginalized notes narrate Black thought, experience, relationship, and ontology, while the synthesis of such ideas showcases the collaborations that Black creators rely on to produce their work and to live as Black—to live in opposition of normative ways of being, thinking, and knowing.
[149] This line references Langston Hughes's 1921 "The Negro Speaks of Rivers."